Getting Ready

A Career as an Internet Designer

by Bill Lund

Content Consultant:
Owen D. Johnson
Webmasters Guild

CAPSTONE PRESS
MANKATO, MINNESOTA

C A P S T O N E   P R E S S
818 North Willow Street • Mankato, Minnesota 56001
http://www.capstone-press.com

Printed in the United States of America.

Library of Congress Cataloging-in-Publication Data
Lund, Bill, 1954-
    Getting ready for a career as an Internet designer/by Bill Lund.
    p. cm.
    Summary: Provides an overview of the development and capabilities of
the Internet and briefly discusses home pages and related careers.
    Includes bibliographical references and index.
    ISBN 1-56065-551-8
    1. Internet (Computer network)--Juvenile literature. 2. Web sites--
Design--Juvenile literature. [1. Internet (Computer network) 2. Programming
(Electronic computers)--Vocational guidance. 3. Vocational guidance.]
I. Title.
TK5105.875.I57L863   1998
004.67'8--dc21

                                            97-12201
                                               CIP
                                               AC

Photo credits
Computer Associates, 24
FPG/Stephen Simpson, 4, 22; Jim Cummins, 7; Michael
    Krasowitz, 8, 47; Adam Smith, 12; Gary Buss, 15; Bill
    Losh, 28; Telegraph Colour Library, 28
Images International/Erwin C. Nielsen, 33
Silicon Graphics, 16, 27, 34
Mike Stokka, cover, 10, 21, 30, 44
Unicorn Stock/Tom McCarthy, 36, 43; Martha McBride,
    38-39

Table of Contents

Chapter 1 A Career on the Internet 5

Chapter 2 Creating a Web Site 13

Chapter 3 Education and Certification 23

Chapter 4 The Changing Internet 31

Photo Diagram 38

Words to Know 40

To Learn More 42

Useful Addresses 45

Internet Sites 46

Index 48

Chapter One

A Career on the Internet

Ten years ago, people used the Internet mostly for science and education. The Internet is a huge network that joins millions of computers. A network is a group of computers that are linked together for communication. Communication is the sharing of information, ideas, or feelings.

Once computers are put on a network, it does not matter where the computers are located. They can communicate whether they are in the same building or thousands of miles apart. The Internet lets people use computers to access information quickly and inexpensively. Access means to exchange information from a computer.

People use the Internet to access information quickly.

5

The number of people using the Internet is growing. Millions of people access the Internet every day.

When few people used the Internet, there were not many Internet careers. But now, more people have careers working with the Internet.

Now, the Internet is used for more than science and education. The Internet has much to offer people who use it. For example, people can play games, find information, listen to music, and watch videos. People access these features by using the World Wide Web.

The World Wide Web

The World Wide Web is a set of software on the Internet that supports pictures, words, music, and movies. Software is a set of programs that tells a computer what to do. A program is a set of instructions that tells a computer what to do. People often shorten the name of the World Wide Web to the Web.

People find information on the Web by visiting Web sites. A site is a place that people can visit on the Web. Each site has its own

The Internet has much to offer people who use it.

6

address. An address is a set of numbers and letters that tells a computer where to go. A person types in a site's address and the computer displays that site on its screen. There are more than 10 million sites on the Internet.

Sites on the Web can contain pictures, movies, sounds, and graphics. The Web is the busiest and fastest-growing part of the Internet.

An Internet designer is a person who creates and maintains Web sites. An Internet designer is usually called a webmaster.

Webmasters' Responsibilities

Webmasters' responsibilities often depend on their experience and training. The jobs they do also depend on the size of their Web sites. Companies require webmasters to have many skills. Webmasters can perform many tasks. Webmasters who have many Internet skills have a greater chance of finding jobs.

Sites can contain many types of information. Webmasters may create the content or decide

---

Companies require webmasters to have many skills.

A webmaster maintains the Web site.

what types of content should be included. Words and pictures are the only content on some Web sites. Other sites include movies and music. Some webmasters create areas on sites where people can place all this information. Each type of content has its own area. Webmasters put movies in one area and words in another area.

Most webmasters make sure Internet users can get around the sites easily. They use programs that help people search sites' contents. They also help people who are having problems visiting the sites or finding information.

Most webmasters keep track of how many people visit their Web sites. They try to make the Web sites as interesting as possible to encourage visitors. If few people visit, webmasters might add new features to the Web sites.

Webmasters also maintain the Web sites. They keep the sites running smoothly. They make sure all of the links work. A link is a connection. It connects users to another part of a site or a completely different site. Broken links are called link rot. Webmasters fix or remove link rot.

Webmasters try to create high-quality Web sites. They make sure information is current and correct. They make sure the sites contain appealing pictures and artwork.

Chapter 2
Creating a Web Site

Ten years ago, there was no webmaster career. Today, the Internet's popularity has made webmaster one of the fastest-growing careers.

A webmaster's responsibilities vary from company to company. Sometimes a webmaster creates a whole site alone. But usually a webmaster is in charge of a team. The team works together to create and control a site's contents.

Sometimes webmasters create a Web site's elements themselves. Other times webmasters manage people who have certain skills. Webmasters may have writers, artists, and people with computer skills on Web-site teams.

A webmaster is usually in charge of a team.

There are three main elements of an Internet site. These elements must work together for a site to be successful.

Writing

Writing is the first element of a Web site. People convey information mainly through words. Information on the Internet is no exception. Sometimes a webmaster or a team member does the writing for a site.

Webmasters or members of the team have good writing skills. They must present information in understandable and interesting ways. A webmaster might also make sure the writing follows a consistent style.

The type of writing done depends on who owns the site. Companies may need writing that advertises products or services. Schools or government sites usually need writing that helps people learn.

Sometimes large companies hire professional writers. A professional is a person who is hired to do something for money.

Webmasters should have good writing skills.

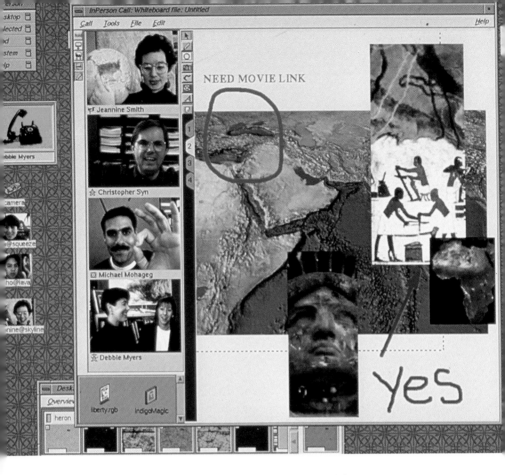

Design is the shape or style of something.

Design

Design is the second element of a Web site.
Design is the shape or style of something.
Webmasters decide where everything will be
placed on a site. They make sure their sites
have an eye-catching design.

Webmasters also work to design their sites logically. Logic means careful and correct reasoning. For example, webmasters usually put titles at the top of a page. That way people know what information the page contains. Webmasters also make sure the pictures go well with the information. Pictures of pigs on a site talking only about horses would be a design mistake.

Graphic elements of a Web site are important, too. A graphic is an image such as a drawing, map, or graph. Many webmasters create the graphics on sites. Some webmasters use graphics they have purchased from outside artists. Sometimes an artist on a Web-site team creates the graphics. Webmasters may choose which graphics to put on a site. They make sure the graphics are colorful and interesting.

People should be able to understand what graphics represent. For example, many sites have different areas to visit. One important area is the home page. A home page is an area that

lists what the entire site contains. Some home pages have links to other parts of a site. Webmasters often use the image of a house to represent a link to the home page.

Webmasters make decisions about the appearance of words on a site, too. They may choose the type style as well as the size and color of the letters. They decide where the words will go on the page.

Some sites have background colors or patterns. Most webmasters select backgrounds that make the rest of the sites look better. They make sure the background does not make the information hard to read.

Programming

The third element of a good Web site is programming. Programming is entering a set of instructions into a computer. The instructions tell a computer what to do. Instructions are written in computer languages. A site needs to be programmed before it will work on the Web.

Some webmasters program computers.

Webmasters must know how to program computers. They should know several computer languages. That way they can program the instructions sites need to work correctly.

Programming becomes more difficult when a site has many features. Then many instructions need to be programmed. If a site has music, the webmaster must program when the music should start and end. A site may also have moving graphics. The webmaster programs the speed at which the graphics move. A webmaster also programs the way graphics move.

Programming becomes more difficult when a site has many features.

20

Chapter Three
Education and Certification

Webmasters learn skills through education and training. After finishing high school, some webmasters become certified. Certified means a person has completed special training to do a certain job.

Education

People who want to become webmasters should finish high school. Taking high school classes in English, math, art, and computers helps future webmasters. These classes give students some background in writing, math, design, and computer skills.

People do not need college degrees to become webmasters. But they do need training

Classes in computers help future webmasters.

in computers, programming, and the Internet. Some people teach themselves about the Internet. But most webmasters need school after high school.

Some webmasters attend technical colleges to receive education and training. A technical college is a school after high school. It offers classes that often include hands-on training for certain jobs.

Other people may choose to attend universities. A university is a school for higher learning after high school. There people can study for degrees or learn about jobs in law or medicine. A degree is a title given by a college. Many future webmasters attend universities and get degrees in computer science.

Webmaster Certificate

In the past, there were no training programs just for webmasters. The Internet was too new. Colleges did not offer classes focusing on the job skills webmasters needed. Now, classes that webmasters need are available.

Many people attend colleges to become webmasters.

Some colleges offer a webmaster training program. Students learn skills such as programming languages and Web-site design. Graduates of the training program receive Webmaster Certificates. The certificates show that students have completed training to be webmasters.

People hoping to become webmasters make the decision whether to become certified. It is often a difficult decision. Many people in the webmaster field disagree on whether certification is needed.

Some employers do not feel people need a Webmaster Certificate to be a good webmaster. These employers look mainly at a person's experience when they decide who to hire. They look at the sites that webmasters have created. The quality of the webmasters' sites shows the webmasters' skill level.

Other employers look at webmasters' experience, too. But some companies prefer to hire webmasters with certificates. Then the

Some employers look at a webmaster's site to judge a webmaster's skills.

Silicon Graphics

NEWS & EVENTS   SEARCH
HELP   HOW TO BUY

SILICON SURF™

WHO
WE ARE

PRODUCTS
& SOLUTIONS

GLOBAL
SITES

CUSTOMER
SUPPORT

TECHNOLOGY
& DEVELOPERS

SERIOUS
FUN

WEB
INNOVATION

Developer
& Cosmo
Forum '96

Moving Worlds Proposal
Voted As VRML 2.0

Cosmo Code 1.0 Available Now

SILICON CAMPUS

Your Resource
For
Education

Developer
Forum '96
Register Now!

ZONE

Attention
Zone Member
Win A T-Shirt

nd your comments to webmaster@www.sgi.com.

employers know exactly what kind of training the webmasters received. They can look at school grades to see whether the webmasters were good students.

In this way, Webmaster Certificates help job-seeking webmasters convince employers to hire them. Webmaster Certificates help assure employers that the webmasters possess skills the companies need.

Some companies hire webmasters with Webmaster Certificates.

Chapter Four

The Changing Internet

The Internet grows very quickly. Every week, thousands of people and businesses start using the Internet. Many of these people hire webmasters to create new sites for them.

People are constantly thinking of new features for sites. Other people invent easier ways to program and access information. People often need webmasters to change and update existing sites.

Keeping Informed

Webmasters spend a lot of time visiting other sites because the Internet changes often. This helps them keep informed about new features on the Internet. The other sites sometimes give

Webmasters often visit other sites.

webmasters new ideas.

Many webmasters read books about new features on the Internet. They read about new design ideas. Some buy magazines about the World Wide Web and popular Web sites. Reading about the changing Internet helps webmasters know about new trends. Some might even take college courses to develop or renew their skills.

New technologies become popular, too. Technology is the use and science of doing practical things. Scientists and engineers redesign computers so the computers work faster. They invent new ways to access the Internet. One new technology allows people to access the Internet with a television.

Businesses want to use the newest technologies. Webmasters working for businesses also need to learn about the new technologies. Some companies offer on-the-job

Scientists and engineers invent new ways for people to access the Internet.

Many businesses use the Internet to sell products.

training in new technologies. Other webmasters might take classes to learn about the new technologies.

Security

Many businesses use the Internet to sell products. Millions of people buy these products. But people must send important personal and financial information through the Internet to buy products. Sometimes people need to send credit card numbers and bank account numbers.

Recently, criminals have found ways to capture this information. Criminals use the information to buy things for themselves.

Some people refuse to buy products from the Internet because of the criminals. Others will only buy products if they know their information is safe. Security is often part of a webmaster's job.

Some webmasters help make sure a person's information is safe. They try to create programs that keep criminals from finding the information. That way criminals will not be able to steal other people's money.

Sometimes people send personal messages to other people. The messages often contain

private information. Webmasters try to create programs that keep messages safe, too. That way other people cannot read what has been written.

The Future

There are many job openings for webmasters. As the Internet grows, so does the number of job opportunities. In the late 1990s, beginning webmasters earned from $35,000 to $50,000. The wage depends on a webmaster's education, training, and experience. Today, there are not enough skilled webmasters to fill the available jobs.

The Internet is making major changes in business, education, and communication. Many people feel the Internet will be the most important communication tool of the future. Skilled webmasters will be in high demand to help create and maintain the Internet. People who become webmasters will work in a constantly growing and changing field.

Many people feel the Internet will be the most important tool of the future.

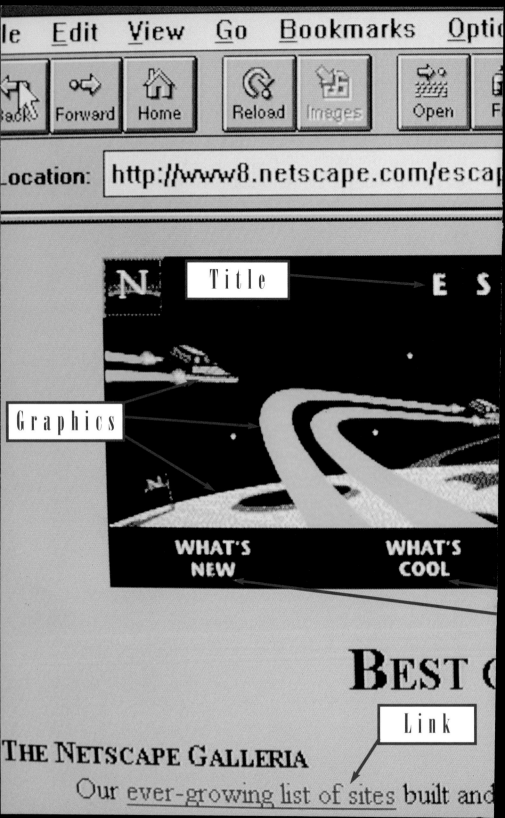

Directory

Stop

dex.html ← **Address**

A P E S

INTERNET DIRECTORY | **INTERNET SEARCH**

Other Areas of Site

THE NET

ed with Netscape Server software. Each

Words to Know

access (AK-sess)—to exchange information from a computer

address (AD-ress)—a set of numbers and letters that tells a computer where to go

degree (di-GREE)—a title given by a college

design (di-ZINE)—the shape or style of something

Internet (IN-tur-net)—a network that joins millions of computers together

link (LINGK)—a connection to another part of a site or a completely different site

logic (LOJ-ik)—careful and correct reasoning

network (NET-wurk)—a group of computers that is linked together to communicate

programming (PROH-gram-ing)—entering a set of instructions into a computer

technical college (TEK-nuh-kuhl KOL-ij)—a school after high school offering classes that often include hands-on training for certain jobs
software (SAWFT-wair)—a set of programs
technology (tek-NOL-uh-jee)—the use and science of doing practical things
university (yoo-nuh-VUR-suh-tee)—a four-year school for higher learning after high school where people can study for degrees
Web site (WEB SITE)—a place people can go on the World Wide Web
World Wide Web (WURLD WIDE WEB)—a set of software on the Internet; often called the Web

To Learn More

Cochrane, Kerry. *The Internet*. New York: Franklin Watts, 1995.

Krol, Ed. *The Whole Internet*. Sebastapol, Cal.: O'Reilly & Associates, Inc., 1992.

Pedersen, Ted and Francis Moss. *Internet for Kids!* New York: Price Stern Sloan, Inc., 1995.

Schepp, Debra and Brad Schepp. *Kidnet: The Kid's Guide to Surfing Through Cyberspace*. New York: HarperCollins, 1996.

Computers on a network can communicate even if they are thousands of miles apart.

Mankato
STATE UNIVERSITY

Academics
Academic Affairs, Colleges, Departments...

Alumni
Alumni Newspaper *Today*, Alur Chapters & Events...

Media & Publications
Catalog, Handbooks, Policies Newspapers...

Administration
Mission, Vision, Org., Policie Offices...

Online Resources
Libraries, Computing Resources, Assistance...

Useful Addresses

Certification of Computing Professionals
2200 East Devon Avenue
Suite 268
Des Plaines, IL 60018

International United Webmasters Association
24 Harley Road
Toms River, NJ 08755

International Webmasters Association
275 South Marengo Avenue, 7
Pasadena, CA 91101

WebMaster
492 Old Connecticut Path
PO Box 9208
Framingham, MA 01701

Sometimes webmasters create sites for universities.

Internet Sites

International United WebMasters Association
http://www.iuwa.org

International Webmasters Association
http://www.irwa.org/index.html

WebMaster Online
http://www.cio.com/WebMaster

Webmasters Guild
http://www.webmaster.org

Every week, thousands of people and businesses start using the Internet.

Index

access, 5, 31, 32
address, 6, 9
artist, 13, 17

background, 19

computer language, 20
criminal, 35

degree, 25
design, 16-17, 23, 26

graphic, 17, 20

home page, 17, 19

link, 11, 19
link rot, 11
logic, 17

maintain, 11

network, 5

professional, 14
program, 3, 6, 20, 37
programming, 19, 20, 25

security, 35
software, 6

technical college, 25
technology, 32, 34
type style, 19

university, 25

wage, 37
Webmaster Certificate, 26,
   29
writer, 13, 14

AC0 8895